EXAMINING POLITICAL SYSTEMS™

COMMUNISM

Xina M. Uhl and Theodore Link

rosen publishing's rosen central

New York

Published in 2020 by The Rosen Publishing Group, Inc.
29 East 21st Street, New York, NY 10010

First Edition

Library of Congress Cataloging-in-Publication Data

Names: Uhl, Xina M. | Link, Theodore, author.
Title: Communism / Xina M. Uhl and Theodore Link.
Description: First edition. | New York : Rosen Central, 2020. | Series: Examining political systems | Includes bibliographical references and index.
Identifiers: LCCN 2018019066| ISBN 9781508184485 (library bound) | ISBN 9781508184478 (pbk.)
Subjects: LCSH: Communism—History—Juvenile literature.
Classification: LCC HX36 .U3947 2019 | DDC 335.43—dc23
LC record available at https://lccn.loc.gov/2018019066

Manufactured in the United States of America

On the cover: Karl Marx (*center, right*) appears next to a German-language version of his groundbreaking work, *The Communist Manifesto* (*center, left*). The end of East German Communism is signaled by the destruction of the Berlin wall (*bottom*).

CONTENTS

INTRODUCTION

People have been trying to create an ideal society for thousands of years. Highly influential thinkers such as the ancient Greek philosopher Plato believed that such a society could be found in Communism. To Plato, this society involved an upper class of specially trained rulers who would live together and share property, spouses, and children. About a thousand years later the English scholar Thomas More came up with a society that had no money, where people shared all property. More called this city-state Utopia. Today the word utopia means a perfect society—one so perfect that it does not exist.

The political and economic system called Communism did not become a major force in the world until the work of a German thinker named Karl Marx. Marx lived in the nineteenth century, when the Industrial Revolution brought great changes to society. These changes included the development of steam engines, internal combustion engines, factories, a steel-making process that allowed for the construction of towering skyscrapers, and the mass movement of people from a farm-based existence to one in crowded cities. The growth of businesses brought wealth and power—but only to a few. Those who worked in the factories, or lived in cramped, dirty tenement houses, suffered from miserable poverty. Marx's book *The Communist Manifesto*, written in 1848, argued that the worker class would rise up and overthrow the power of the wealthy. Marx's book inspired a large following around the world, including in Russia, where Communism first took root.

Chairman Mao Tse-tung (*second from left*) of China reviews an honor guard upon his arrival at the Moscow airport in 1957. He is accompanied by the Union of Soviet Socialist Republic's (USSR) chief of staff Marshall Kliment Yefremovich Voroshilov.

During World War I, Russia's government dissolved. An exile named Vladimir Lenin took over, and established a dictatorship in which the government owned almost all industry. Large farms were created and distributed to groups of peasants. The next Russian dictator, Joseph Stalin, ruled Russia with complete power. Stalin's people suffered mass starvation under his changes to the government, which involved more establishments of peasant farm collectives.

The end of World War II found Russia and the United States at odds. Russia favored the expansion of their form of Communism, and the United States was determined to stop this expansion and promote democracy instead. The Cold

War developed between both powers, a rivalry that played out across the world in policies, governments, and economic ideas. The rivalry would end in the late twentieth century, but remnants of it remain to this day.

China embraced Communism as well. A civil war in 1945 put Mao Tse-tung in control. Greatly influenced by Lenin's theories of Communism, Mao undertook massive changes in China's economy and government. The result pushed China toward a higher degree of industrialization. It also resulted in an iron-tight grip upon the Chinese people that led to mass starvation and the imprisonment and execution of those who disagreed with the government.

The last remaining country to practice USSR-style Communism is North Korea. The conclusion of World War II led to a division between North and South Korea and the international struggle of the Korean War. South Korea emerged from the war with a democratic republican form of government that conflicts with North Korea's Communist ideals. While the twentieth century saw the greatest number of Communist governments, some still linger in the world—and so does their influence upon others.

CHAPTER 1

BEGINNINGS OF COMMUNISM

Democracy came from the ancient Greeks, and so did Communism. Greek philosophers and thinkers, such as Plato, envisioned a golden age of Communism, in which private property did not exist and people lived together in peace and harmony.

THE IDEAL GOVERNMENT

The Greek philosopher Plato (ca. 428–ca. 347 BCE) outlined his own ideas for a perfect government in a work called *Republic*. Written as a dialogue led by the great teacher Socrates, Plato intended it to teach his students about justice. *Republic's*

This marble head of Plato dates from between the fourth and first centuries BCE. One of the best known and most influential of the Greek philosophers, Plato founded the Academy in Athens.

COMMUNAL LIVING

Religious orders took up the notion of communal living. Early Christian groups such as the Gnostics and Manichaeans believed that private property was evil and that the whole earth was for the use of all people. More communal orders arose as Christianity spread. The Franciscans also believed in working for the good of the group over the individual.

Groups belonging to other religions also practiced communal living. An early Jewish order called the Essenes believed in a highly organized society based on shared property. They viewed trade as evil. In the Americas, the Incas built an empire based on the idea of communal property and labor. Many other tribes shared their disdain for private property.

characters proposed a society ruled by wise thinkers called philosopher-kings.

In *Republic*, an elite level of educated warriors called guardians protected their imagined city. The city provided all citizens with ample food, clothing, and shelter. The guardians shared family responsibility, homes, and food. Private property stopped existing for the guardians. They became more capable defenders when freed from these distractions. Everyone happily served the city's needs. Communal property ensured that the philosopher-kings ruled the city for the interests of the people, not to serve their own greed. While Plato's dream city never came to exist, his ideas influenced Europe in the coming years.

THE DREAM OF UTOPIA

As Europe passed into the Middle Ages, a form of government called the manorial system evolved. The Middle Ages, lasting

This woodcut, entitled *The Island of Utopia*, appeared as an illustration in the third edition of Sir Thomas More's *Utopia*. It depicts the fictional island of Utopia as More might have imagined it. It was created in 1518 by German artist Ambrosius Holbein.

from 400 to 1499 CE, marked a general decline in European society. Under the manorial system, landlords owned the land while peasants worked the fields. Much of the yield from the harvest went to the landlord as rent. The peasants worked the land together to lessen the burden on each person. Villages often contained a plot of land called the commons. Every community member worked in the commons, and the food grown there belonged to all who shared the labor. The lords and nobles sometimes tried to take over village commons, but the peasants resisted. They were willing to fight for this common land. Conflicts led to the Peasant's Revolt in England in 1381 and the Peasant's War fought in Germany during the sixteenth century.

In 1516, a writer and adviser to England's King Henry VIII named Thomas More published a book called *Utopia*. Describing a wonderful country to his readers, More imagined himself traveling to the nation of Utopia as an ambassador for Henry VIII. There, he and his companions witnessed a society that organized everything in the best interests of humanity.

People who read or heard *Utopia* read aloud were excited to hear that the Utopians did not have to work constantly. More wrote that Utopians did not: "wear themselves out with perpetual toil, from morning to night, as if they were beasts of burden, which, as it is indeed a heavy slavery, so it is everywhere the common course of life among all mechanics except the Utopians; but they dividing the day and night into twenty-four hours, appoint six of these for work." The rest of their time was devoted to eating, sleeping, and what More called "proper exercise," which usually meant reading or attending lectures.

More pointed out that the Utopians had plenty of food to eat and clothing to wear while working for only six hours. Their production was greater because all women and men shared the burden of labor. More pointed out that in England:

> if all those who labor about useless things were set to more profitable employments, and if all they that languish out their lives in sloth and idleness, every one of whom consumes as much as any two of the men that are at work, were forced to labor, you may easily imagine that a small proportion of time would serve for doing all that is either necessary, profitable, or pleasant to mankind.

The Utopians wore clothing that they made themselves, did not care about accumulating wealth, and lived in buildings "so uniform that a whole side of a street looks like one house." More's Utopians had much in common with Plato's guardians in terms of property and division of labor. However, More believed in keeping distinct family units whole. Plato wanted every citizen to be every other citizen's parent or sibling.

Citizens governed Utopia democratically. Thirty families elected an official to govern them called a philarch. Every ten philarchs selected an archphilarch to rule over them. The people in each of the four sections of a Utopian city chose a candidate for the office of prince. All two hundred philarchs voted to choose the prince, the highest authority of the city, from these four candidates. All officials except for the prince had term limits. More wrote that, "The Prince is for life, unless he is removed upon suspicion of some design to enslave the people."

Thomas More never attempted to establish a society like the one described in his book, but the idea intrigued many other thinkers. Other authors wrote similar books. The word "utopia" eventually came to mean any idealistic community.

This portrait of Robert Owen was created around 1810. Owen was one of the three men considered to be the primary forerunners of modern Communist thought.

UTOPIAS EVOLVE

Later thinkers did try to bring More's ideas to life. A British man named Robert Owen made an ambitious attempt to start a utopian community. When the Industrial Revolution began in Great Britain during the eighteenth century, people crowded into cities to find jobs in factories. They often worked long hours in miserable conditions for little pay. The large number of people looking for jobs enabled factory owners to hire people for low wages and fire them when they pleased. Many people suffered sickness and injuries caused by poor working conditions.

A manufacturer himself, Owen bought several mills in Scotland. He built communities around them for workers, complete with good housing and sanitation, schools, and stores whose earnings went back into the community. Production at his mills increased along with the quality of life enjoyed by his workers. Owen also founded utopian communities in the United States, most famously at New Harmony in Indiana.

These failed when Owen and his partners disagreed over their management.

Back in Great Britain, Owen helped to pass a workers' rights law in 1819, slightly improving working conditions. Many of Owen's early ideas were outlined in his collection of essays, *A New View of Society*. There, he outlined what he saw as a novel way to improve the lives of workers everywhere. The cornerstone of Owen's early thought was education. He wrote, "Train any population rationally, and they will be rational. Furnish honest and useful employments to those so trained, and such employments they will greatly prefer to dishonest or injurious occupations." Owen felt that everyone needed an education. The government should provide education and also help unemployed workers. Later in life, Owen worked to start labor unions, organizations of workers. By joining together, the workers could lobby for improvements in working conditions for their fellow union members.

CHAPTER 2

COMMUNISTS EMERGE

Socialism developed out of the ideas put forth by Utopian thinkers. While Socialism occurred inside an existing government, it involved people within a society gathered in communes and shared property and responsibilities.

REFINERS OF COMMUNIST THOUGHT

Robert Owen envisioned the world peacefully making the transition to his form of Socialism by following the example of his communities. He dreamed of workers coming together in their cooperatives. Wealthy capitalists would no longer own all of the factories and land, known as the “means of production.” Instead, the workers would become joint owners. Communists shared many views with socialists but felt governments could make the transition only through revolution.

Communists saw a social system divided into classes. The bourgeoisie were the middle-class capitalists who owned the means of production. Below them were the petit-bourgeoisie. These were made up of shopkeepers, tradesmen, artisans, and peasants who made money by providing goods necessary for life and comfort. The bottom rung was made up by the proletariat, poor people who owned no property. The proletariat worked for the bourgeoisie in factories.

FRANÇOIS BABEUF

François Babeuf is often recognized as the father of Communism in Europe. He emerged after the French Revolution overthrew King Louis XVI and brought democracy to France. In his *Manifesto of the Equals*, published in 1796, he argued that the French Revolution had not gone far enough in creating political equality. Babeuf believed that all people should be economic equals as well and that private property caused people to organize into masters and slaves. His society would divide property equally. He wrote:

> Vanish at last, revolting distinctions of rich and poor, of great and small, of masters and servants, of governors and governed. Let there be no difference between men than that of age and sex. Since all have the same needs and the same faculties, let there be only one education, one kind of food.

Babeuf spent time in a prison for his writings. He later formed a secret society that plotted to

Also known as Gracchus Babeuf, François Babeuf, son of a farmer, ran a journal called *Le Correspondant picard* in which he proposed radical land reforms during the French Revolution.

overthrow the government. The government discovered this Conspiracy of the Equals and executed Babeuf in 1797.

MARX AND ENGELS

Karl Marx and Friedrich Engels took inspiration from both Robert Owen's social communes and François Babeuf's vision of a proletariat uprising. Born into a middle-class family in Germany, Karl Marx studied law briefly before switching to philosophy. He worked as a journalist, writing Socialist commentary until moving to Paris in 1843. There, he met Friedrich Engels, the son of a wealthy English manufacturer. Engels had become a Socialist after observing the horrible working conditions at his father's factories. Together, they began working on ideas that would later become the basis for modern Communism.

Exiled from Paris in 1845, Marx traveled to Belgium. He joined with a collection of artisans who called themselves the Communist League. In 1847, the Communist League was plotting a workers' revolution. The members commissioned Marx and Engels to write an article detailing their goals and beliefs. Marx and Engels

Karl Marx is considered the main architect of modern Communism. His writings continue to be a main source of reference for Communists and Socialists throughout the world.

began working on *The Communist Manifesto*. The pressures on them to write a document with mass appeal were staggering. Engels later wrote that "in 1847, Socialism was a middle-class movement; Communism a working-class movement. Socialism was, on the continent at least, 'respectable': Communism was the very opposite."

THE DIVISION OF LABOR

In the opening lines of *The Communist Manifesto*, Marx declared that Europe's ruling powers saw Communism as a threat: "A spectre is haunting Europe—the spectre of Communism. All the powers of old Europe have entered into a holy alliance to exorcise this spectre." Marx moved forward to describe history as the history of class struggles. He wrote, "Our epoch, the epoch of the bourgeoisie, possesses, however, this distinctive feature: it has simplified the class antagonisms. Society as a whole is more and more splitting up into two great hostile camps, into two great classes directly facing each other—bourgeoisie and proletariat."

To Marx, the Industrial Revolution caused the evolution of the two classes. Factory owners

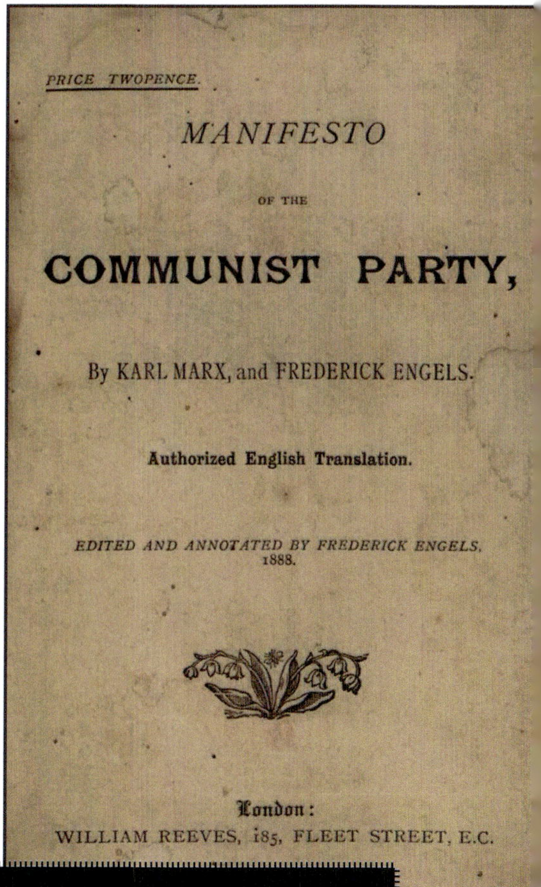

The Communist Manifesto has been printed in numerous languages since its first publication. The first authorized English version is pictured here. See page 52 for a partial transcription.

gained profits by spending as little as possible on production and selling more of the finished product. He wrote, "The bourgeoisie during its rule of scarce one hundred years has created more massive and more colossal productive forces than have all preceding generations together."

Before the Industrial Revolution, independent craftsmen and guild members earned a living by selling carefully handcrafted items. This changed after the colonization of the New World and the rise of factories. Goods had to be produced much faster to be sent to the colonies. Instead of a single craftsman creating a single piece, many unskilled workers contributed to the finished product. Production sped up with many people performing one task they knew well on many items.

The wages of the unskilled factory workers were much lower than those of the skilled craftsmen. The craftsmen charged more for labor because they knew how to produce the entire item. Factory workers knew only how to do their one part. Marx described the relationship between the bourgeoisie and the proletariat as one of exploitation. He blasted the bourgeoisie for turning most of society into wage earners with no choice but to serve the existing system: "The bourgeoisie has stripped of its halo every occupation hitherto honoured and looked up to with reverent awe. It has converted the priest, the poet, the man of science, into its paid wage labourers."

Marx condemned the effects of factory labor on the worker when he wrote: "

> Owing to the extensive use of machinery and to divisions of labor, the work of the proletarians has lost all individual character, and consequently, all charm for the workman. He becomes an appendage of the machine, and is only the most simple, most monotonous, and most easily acquired knack that is required of him.

He compared wage laborers to an army serving a hierarchy of managers, calling them slaves of the bourgeoisie.

According to Marx, the petit-bourgeoisie also resisted the wealthier factory owners, "to save from extinction their existence as fractions of the middle class." The petit-bourgeoisie only struggled against the bourgeoisie because they did not want to slip into the lower-class proletariat.

A CALL FOR REVOLUTION

The proletariat could only free itself from its position of servitude to the bourgeoisie through revolution. In its greed for money, the middle class created a class of dependent wage earners much larger than itself. "What the bourgeoisie, therefore, produces above all are its own grave-diggers. Its fall and the victory of the proletariat are equally inevitable," wrote Marx.

Marx proposed that the Communist Party take a position of leadership in this revolution and create an international movement. The proletariat revolution hoped to erase social classes.

A first step toward this new equality would ban private property. Critics of Communism claim that taking away or dividing hard-earned property is unjust. Marx replied that wage labor does not create property for the workers, but only capital.

The wage laborer had nothing to exchange for property except work time. Under the system dominated by the bourgeoisie, their time became capital, paid regularly. The capital allowed the laborer only the means of subsistence. Workers did not earn enough capital to buy property and did not have the time to work toward bettering their position.

Marx wrote that few people really have private property at all: "You are horrified at our intending to do away with private property. But in your existing society private property is already done away with for nine-tenths of the population; its existence for the few is solely due to its non-existence in the hands of those nine-tenths."

Critics raised concerns that a Communist government would eliminate education and the institution of the family. Marx replied that it would end the exploitation of children by their parents and the influence of the bourgeoisie over education. Under the bourgeoisie system, children worked in factories and were "transformed into simple articles of commerce and instruments of labour." Marx's Communist government would destroy all divisions of labor. Every worker would be educated in many different kinds of work. As workers took control of governments and the old social order toppled, even national boundaries would gradually vanish.

Marx addressed the system of classes that placed the bourgeoisie at the top of the social order and the proletariat at the bottom. Throughout history, social classes have struggled against each other. These struggles always end in the dominance of one class over another. Over time, the new social order would be overturned and another one would rise in its place.

Communism would end the cycle by creating a classless society. Marx finished *The Communist Manifesto* with strong words of encouragement for Communists and workers everywhere when he wrote, "Let the ruling classes tremble at a Communist revolution. The proletarians have nothing to lose but their chains. They have a world to win. Workingmen of all countries, unite!"

THE MOVEMENT GROWS

The revolutions foretold by Marx and Engels began all across Europe in 1848, but they all encountered problems. Little coordination existed between the revolutionary groups. Most national armies remained loyal to their old rulers and easily put down the revolts. Marx himself was tried for treason. Acquitted,

BAKUNIN AND REVOLUTIONARY SOCIALISM

Over time, rifts appeared in the International. Working conditions in factories had gradually improved. As news of the Paris Commune's failure sank in, Marx began rethinking the logic of a worldwide revolt. He took greater control of the International and steered it toward a more gradual program of change.

Some Communists followed Marx, but others preferred the leadership of Mikhail Bakunin. Bakunin believed strongly in the dissolution of all national governments. He called his movement Revolutionary Socialism. He considered the Communists' new focus on political revolution unreasonable. He and his group, labeled Anarchists, participated in the congress of the International Workingman's Association in Basel, Switzerland, in 1869. They attempted to steer the congress and therefore the International toward their views but were voted down. Bakunin set down the Revolutionary Socialists' agenda in his essay "Marxism, Freedom, and the State," written between 1870 and 1872. They would "organise with a view to the destruction, or if you prefer a politer word, the liquidation of the State."

Friedrich Engels recognized the threat Bakunin and the Anarchists posed to the Communist movement. In a letter he wrote to Theodor Cuno on January 24, 1872, Engels established the differences between the two ideologies. Anarchism worked to destroy governments, while Communism wished to use them to better the lot of workers until a time when they become unnecessary.

he was expelled from Prussia. The next two decades saw Communism dwindle in Europe.

MARX AND THE FIRST INTERNATIONAL

Marx remained influential in the Communist movement. His writings inspired the foundation of the International Workingman's Party in 1864. The goal of the International, as it was called, was

Soldiers at the Rue Castiglione brace themselves for conflict during the uprising of the French proletariat. With Prussian help, the French recaptured Paris and executed thousands of rebels.

to establish the means for another workers' revolution. Marx eventually became head of the International Workingman's Party. Though Communists established parties all over the world, the International could not get its revolution off the ground.

Communists had some success in France. In 1871, the French government collapsed after losing the Franco-German War. Citizens of Paris elected a radical government. This elected government set about turning Paris into a commune. In defiance of the national government, which had fled to Versailles, the elected commune began instituting economic and social changes throughout the city. It outlawed child labor, established a minimum wage, and reopened factories. Communists hailed the Paris Commune as a first step toward a "Universal Social Republic." The French government sent its army to crush the commune. The army attacked on May 21, 1871 and took control of the city on May 28 after a ferocious siege called Bloody Week. Paris remained under martial law for five years afterward and banned the International Workingman's Party.

Mikhail Bakunin took Marx's ideas to a new level in Revolutionary Socialism, which opposed national governments altogether. He and his followers were kicked out of the International in 1872 but remained powerful. Feeling increasingly threatened by Bakunin's growing influence, Marx dissolved the International Workingman's Party in 1876. The heads of Communist and Socialist groups still asked his advice, but Marx's days as an organizer were over. He died in 1883.

ANOTHER INTERNATIONAL

The Communist movement kept progressing despite Marx's clashes with Bakunin. Though governments grew even more hostile toward any type of Communism or Socialism after the bloody fall of the Paris Commune, Communists continued to organize political parties. In Germany, a Marxist group formed the German Social Democratic Party. The German government responded by making Socialism illegal until 1890. Communists felt the need for a Second International.

The Second, or Socialist, International was established in 1889. The German Social Democratic Party and its Russian counterpart dominated the political wing. Its goal was to bring about change within existing systems of government, rather than through violent revolution. Its leaders, including Friedrich Engels, sought to increase the strength of social democratic movements.

The Second International began to decline around 1900. The revolutionary elements of the Russian Social Democratic Party agitated against the International's moderate approach. The Second International remained influential until 1914, when many of its members supported their native countries at the onset of the First World War. Their patriotism went against the Second International's goal of promoting peace and caused its end.

The Communist revolution, when it came, would have certain requirements according to Marx and Engels. The revolution would need an industrialized nation with factories that generated a surplus of goods. Maintaining this surplus would serve to erase class distinctions. But their predictions took an unexpected turn. Communism first took hold in the poor, agrarian country of Russia.

The Russian Social Democratic Party formed secretly at an 1898 congress in Minsk. At that time, oppressive czars had ruled Russia for centuries. Efforts to overthrow the czars often resulted in brutal retaliation.

Vladimir Lenin was the first leader of the USSR, also known as the Soviet Union. He is primarily responsible for transforming Russia into a Communist nation.

LENIN AND THE REVOLUTION

Lenin was born Vladimir Ilyich Ulyanov in the city of Simbirsk in 1870. The son of a minor government official, Lenin distingushed himself for his revolutionary activities while at the University of Kazan. There, he began studying the writings of Karl Marx and absorbing the idea of a workers' revolution.

Lenin became a full-time revolutionary by the mid-1890s. The government exiled him to the frigid Siberian countryside in 1895 for organizing workers. He left Russia when his exile ended in 1900, probably adopting the name "Lenin" around this time to disguise his identity while traveling through Europe.

In 1902, Lenin published a pamphlet entitled *What Is to Be Done? Burning Questions of Our Movement*. It outlined Lenin's beliefs about how to begin the revolution and create a Communist state. He stated that the proletariat needed outside leadership. They could organize against their bosses and pass labor laws but would not be able to bring about a full-scale revolution. They needed the intellectual community to guide them on the correct path for forming a workers' state.

He recognized the various struggles that had to take place for the Social Democrats to gain power, and he wanted to form a revolutionary Social-Democratic party separate from the workers' groups. Lenin believed in creating a small, secret revolutionary organization made of trained and experienced revolutionaries, ready to fight the military as the workers seized land and factories.

BOLSHEVIKS

Lenin presented the ideas within *What Is to Be Done?* at the Second Congress of the Russian Social Democratic Labor Party,

This is a propaganda poster entitled "All Forces to the Defense of the City of Lenin." Socialist realism, a new art movement, began under the Soviet government and depicted many factory scenes.

held in London in 1903. The party split into two factions. The Bolsheviks agreed with Lenin and his views and soon gained control of the party.

On January 22, 1905, a group of two hundred thousand unarmed workers marched to Saint Petersburg's Winter Palace to present a petition to Czar Nicolas II. Guards opened fire on the crowd, killing or wounding hundreds. This massacre began the short Revolution of 1905. Strikes and demonstrations were held all over the country to protest the crackdown. Mutinies occurred in the armed forces. Peasant uprisings took place in the countryside.

Czar Nicholas II (*center, second from right*) appears with his wife beside him, surrounded by their children. Nicholas and his family were assassinated in 1918. He was the last emperor that Russia would ever have.

Nicolas II tried to calm Russian citizens. He formed an elected legislative body called the Duma to participate in the government. Lenin and the Bolsheviks wanted nothing short of a total overthrow of Russia's monarchy. In 1912 Lenin announced that he was breaking away from the Russian Social Democratic Labor Party to form his own Bolshevik Party.

END OF THE CZARS

When World War I broke out in 1914, Lenin worked even harder to bring about his revolution. Russia had entered the war on the side of France and Great Britain, pitting it against Germany and Austria-Hungary. Most Communists and Socialists supported their countries, but Lenin wanted his country to lose the war. He felt Russia's defeat could lead to the revolution he wanted.

Lenin viewed the entire struggle as a war between the world's imperial powers, fighting to extend the reach of capitalism. He stated that nations fighting in the First World War hoped to extend their imperial territory, specifically calling out Germany, Great Britain, and the United States. He claimed that imperialism expanded the wealth and power of the bourgeoisie. This gave them more freedom to exploit and corrupt the proletariat. Lenin urged the proletariat in all of the countries involved to resist these bribes and revolt.

In 1917, rioting broke out in Saint Petersburg (renamed Petrograd in 1914) and quickly spread. A committee formed by liberal members of the Duma declared itself the Provisional Government of Russia and the czar abdicated the throne on March 2, leaving the committee to rule the country.

Lenin, in Switzerland, heard about these events. He traveled to Petrograd in early April, ready to further the revolution. There, he delivered his famous "April Theses" speech. He called the Provisional Government imperialist and demanded that power be concentrated in the Soviets. To Lenin, any other form of government would be too easily corrupted. The April Theses suggested that all land be confiscated and used for the public good; that the police, military, and bureaucracy be disbanded; and that the Soviets take over production and distribution of products.

Soldiers and workers supported the Bolsheviks. On October 6, 1917, the Russian military staged a coup that placed the Bolsheviks in power. They set up a cabinet called the Council of People's Commissars with Lenin as chairman. Other council members included Leon Trotsky, who organized the coup, and Joseph Stalin. The council immediately abolished private property and divided private and church lands among the people. Over the next several days the October Revolution spread to Moscow.

Yet Lenin's long awaited revolution was tainted. The Bolshevik secret police force, called the Cheka, violently put down opposition. Lenin dissolved councils when Bolsheviks did not have a majority.

The Bolshevik Party became the Russian Communist Party in March 1918. It faced a major crisis that summer. Russian opposition forces, called the

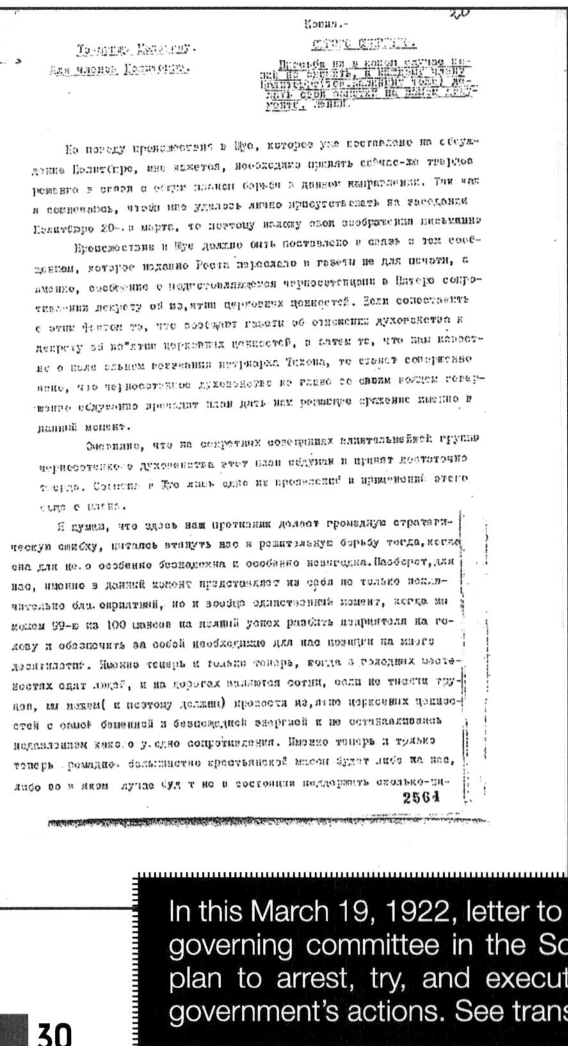

In this March 19, 1922, letter to members of the Politburo, the main governing committee in the Soviet Union, Lenin outlines a brutal plan to arrest, try, and execute church leaders opposed to his government's actions. See transcription on pages 52–53.

A NEW TERM

The word *soviet* derives from the Greek word *symboulion*, or "council of advisers." The term literally means advice or council. It came to represent the Soviet Union's basic governmental unit at all levels. A soviet is an elected local committee that is theoretically made up of workers. It serves as a political representative body, similar to a city council. Soviets were created under Czar Nicholas II as a way of giving peasants a limited voice in government. Communist revolutionaries used soviets as a way to build opposition to the czarist government.

White Army, organized to oust the new government. Leon Trotsky formed an army for the Russian Communist Party called the Red Army. The Russian Civil War lasted until 1921. Lenin also responded to the opposition by beginning the Red Terror. This campaign eliminated political opponents among Russia's citizens. He nationalized factories, managed by strict codes of conduct for the workers. Grain and other crops were seized from the countryside to feed the army and workers in the city. He called these measures War Communism.

THE COMINTERN

Lenin organized the Third International, called the Communist International or Comintern, in March of 1919. The Third International initially saw Europe as the starting point for the international revolution. It soon switched its attention to Asia, encouraging people living in the colonies to revolt against their European colonizers.

This portrait of Joseph Stalin was issued to celebrate his seventieth birthday in 1949. It is believed that Stalin's rough upbringing contributed to his later image as a hardened revolutionary.

Back in Russia, War Communism was wrecking the economy. Strikes and demonstrations became common. In 1921, Lenin introduced a measure called the New Economic Policy, designed to revitalize the economy. It allowed farmers to sell some of their surpluses, lease their land, and put some small businesses back in the hands of private owners.

Lenin suffered a stroke in May of 1922. That month, the Soviet government established the Union of Soviet Socialist Republics, or USSR. It included Russia and several neighboring countries occupied by the Red Army during the war. Lenin wanted a body of leaders to govern the USSR after his death. He blamed his general secretary, Joseph Stalin, for many of the problems facing the USSR. After Lenin died in January 1924, however, Stalin emerged as supreme leader of the Communist Party and the USSR.

STALIN COMES TO POWER

After the October Revolution of 1917, Joseph Stalin took an important post in Lenin's council. He headed the Commissariat for Nationality Affairs, which tried to hold together all of the territories of the old Russian Empire. After the Bolsheviks emerged victorious in 1921, Stalin was elected general secretary of the Communist Party. This position put him in charge of appointing officials. Stalin used his new power to place friends within the government and the party. He managed to suppress the misgivings Lenin had written about him.

Stalin abolished Lenin's New Economic Policy in 1928, declaring that it no longer worked. He replaced it with a program called the Five-Year Plan. Stalin designed the plan to bring about rapid industrial growth in Russia. It forced peasants off their land and onto large collective farms, exploiting their labor to help the

This political cartoon portrays Soviet strongman Joseph Stalin standing on a book by Karl Marx, in which several bodies are crushed. Stalin ruled the Soviet Union for nearly thirty years.

factories grow. Russia transformed itself into an industrialized nation, but millions starved to death in the process.

The Five-Year Plan brought some benefits to peasants. Russia's literacy rate increased and the government provided free medical services. The Five-Year Plan was later extended several times.

Controls over daily life became stricter. It became illegal to criticize public policy. Stalin limited the people's freedom of movement. The secret police arrested and executed thousands of party members who Stalin viewed as potential enemies. These purges increased and spread to the military and civilians. Between 1936 and 1938, the secret police executed between one and seven million people. Millions of others were sent to work in forced labor camps. As a result of the "Great Purge," Stalin's officials were loyal to him alone. Stalin felt that perfection of the USSR would lead to international revolution. To him, democratic measures within the government went against the Communist state's best interests.

CHAPTER 4

COMMUNISM IN ASIA AND BEYOND

World War II raged mainly in Europe and Japan from 1939 until 1945, playing democratic, fascist, Communist, and totalitarian governments against one another until the Allies ultimately prevailed as winners. Meanwhile, a Communist revolt had been underway in China for years, led by a man named Mao Tse-tung.

MAO TSE-TUNG

Mao Tse-tung was born in 1893. The son of peasants living in China's rural Hunan province, Mao was educated in Chinese literary and philosophical classics. He studied Western philosophy in college. Upon graduating in 1918, he moved to Beijing to work in a library. During this time, he began studying Marxist theory and publishing articles criticizing traditional Chinese values.

After failing to set up a democratic government in Hunan, Mao traveled to Shanghi in 1921. There, he was present for the

This poster, entitled "We Wish Mao a Long Life," shows Mao Tse-tung in 1968. Pictures of Mao appeared almost everywhere, portraying him as a sort of savior of the Chinese people.

founding meeting of the Chinese Communist Party (CCP). Mao returned to Hunan and founded a branch of the CCP. He began organizing workers' strikes.

The CCP allied itself with the Kuomintang (KMT) party in 1923. The KMT formed in 1912 after a revolution toppled China's imperial government. Its members believed in moderate Socialism. In 1928, KMT leader Chiang Kai-shek launched a violent purge against the CCP.

From 1928 until 1931, Mao and other CCP leaders organized Soviets in rural China and built an army. They established a Soviet Republic of China based in Jiangxi province with Mao as chairman. Mao and his army developed guerilla tactics designed to draw KMT forces into ambushes. Mao and his Red Army continued battling Chiang Kai-shek's KMT army even as Japanese forces attacked China during the Second Sino-Japanese War (1937–1945). The civil war ended in 1949 with China under CCP control. That year, Mao became chairman of the central government committee of the newly formed People's Republic of China.

Mao organized the People's Republic of China based on the example set by the USSR. In 1957, he launched a program called the Great Leap Forward. The plan attempted to industrialize the country without centralizing industrial power. He built thousands of tiny backyard steel mills throughout China and communalized farmlands. Mao intended to produce raw industrial materials throughout the countryside, allowing industries to grow up beside farms.

Mao described the Chinese path to industrialization in his essay "The Correct Handling of Contradictions Among the People." He wrote, "As China is a large agricultural country, with over 80 percent of her population in the rural areas, industry must develop together with agriculture, for only thus can industry secure raw materials and a market, and only thus is it possible to accumulate fairly large funds for building a heavy industry."

Mao's Great Leap Forward failed miserably. About twenty million people starved in China between 1957 and 1959 due to poor planning. The Soviet Union cut off aid following the disaster. Mao gave up his chairmanship of the central government council but remained chairman of the CCP. He and his supporters launched the Cultural Revolution in 1966. They persecuted his enemies and staged uprisings designed to bring Mao's beliefs back to the fore of China's government. They established a godlike aura around him. All Chinese were encouraged to read *Quotations of Chairman Mao*, commonly called Mao's Little Red Book. Mao died in 1976, and his followers declared the end of the Cultural Revolution.

THE DOMINO THEORY

One of the major reasons for the United States to become involved in the Vietnam War was a principle that became known as the Domino Theory. As President Dwight D. Eisenhower explained, the spread of Communism was like a line of dominos. When one country fell to Communism, it would influence the nearest country to fall in much the same way that standing dominos are toppled when one is knocked over, causing a chain reaction. Eisenhower believed that losing Vietnam to the Communists would cause other countries in southeast Asia such as Cambodia, Laos, and Thailand to fall as well. Eisenhower said that the consequences of such a loss would be "incalculable to the free world."

NORTH KOREA

During World War II, Korea had been occupied by Japan. When the war ended, the United States and the Soviet Union divided the country. The Soviets installed a pro-Communist North Korean Provisional People's Committee in the northern zone in 1946. This body worked on land reform and nationalizing business until 1947. That year, it gave way to the Supreme People's Committee, which was selected by voters from a list of Communist-approved candidates. This legislative body in turn chose Kim Il Sung as North Korea's premier in 1948.

Kim attempted to impose Communism on South Korea as well, touching off the Korean War (1950–1953). China offered aid to North Korea, while the United States and other democratic countries supported South Korea.

The war ended in a stalemate and further widened the split between the two Koreas. After the war, Kim expanded North Korea's heavy industry an organized the country's agricultural interests around collective farming.

VIETNAM

In 1945, the Vietnamese Communist leader Ho Chi Minh (1892–1969) organized the Viet Minh, a league dedicated to winning Vietnam's independence from France. The Viet Minh established the Democratic Republic of Vietnam (DRV), with Ho Chi Minh as president. The French resisted, resulting in the Indo-China War of 1946 to 1954. The signing of the Geneva Accords in 1954 ended the war and split the country into northern and southern halves. Ho Chi Minh became president of the DRV in the Communist-controlled northern half of the country. The southern half, called the Republic of Vietnam (ROV), was governed by an anti-Communist regime.

In 1959, Communist guerillas began attacking targets in South Vietnam, hoping to overthrow its US-supported government. The United States military became involved in 1964 in what would be called the Vietnam War. North Vietnamese forces brought the war to a close in 1975 by capturing Saigon, the South Vietnamese capital. They renamed it Ho Chi Minh City and reunified the country as the Socialist Republic of Vietnam in 1976.

ALBANIA

Italian forces invaded the Balkan country of Albania in 1939, deposing King Zog I. Albanians formed the Communist-led National Liberation front (NLF) in 1941 to resist the Italians and the Germans who took their place in 1943. The NLF succeeded in driving German forces out of the country. The NLF changed its name to the Democratic Front and assumed control of the country. Albania held elections in December 1945, with voters choosing from a list of Communist candidates approved by the Democratic Front.

The government adopted a Soviet-style constitution in March 1946 and established the Party of Labour of Albania as the only legal political party. The party instituted land reform measures and nationalized businesses. It also developed a close relationship with the Soviet Union. When the alliance sourced in 1961, the Soviets broke off diplomatic ties with Albania. In turn, Albania developed ties with Mao Tse-tung's China. When that relationship ended in 1978, Albania experienced isolation and crushing poverty.

Throughout 1991, anti-Communism demonstrators clamored for a new government. Communism in Albania officially came to an end when free elections were held in March 1992.

CHAPTER 5

COMMUNISM'S SPREAD AND IMPACT

The end of World War II seemed to signal the rise of Communism far and wide. The Soviet Union sponsored Communist movements in Asia and South America, and Mao Tse-tung's revolution in China was deeply rooted. However, these movements were short-lived, and most had disintegrated by the end of the twentieth century.

THE DIVISION OF GERMANY

After the war ended, the Allies divided Germany into four zones, occupied by the USSR, France, the United States, and Britain. They also split Berlin in half. Soon, growing mutual distrust between the United States and the USSR increased tensions. The United States feared that the USSR was trying to expand its territory. When Stalin's troops drove the Nazis from Poland, he set up a Communist-friendly government over objections from the United States.

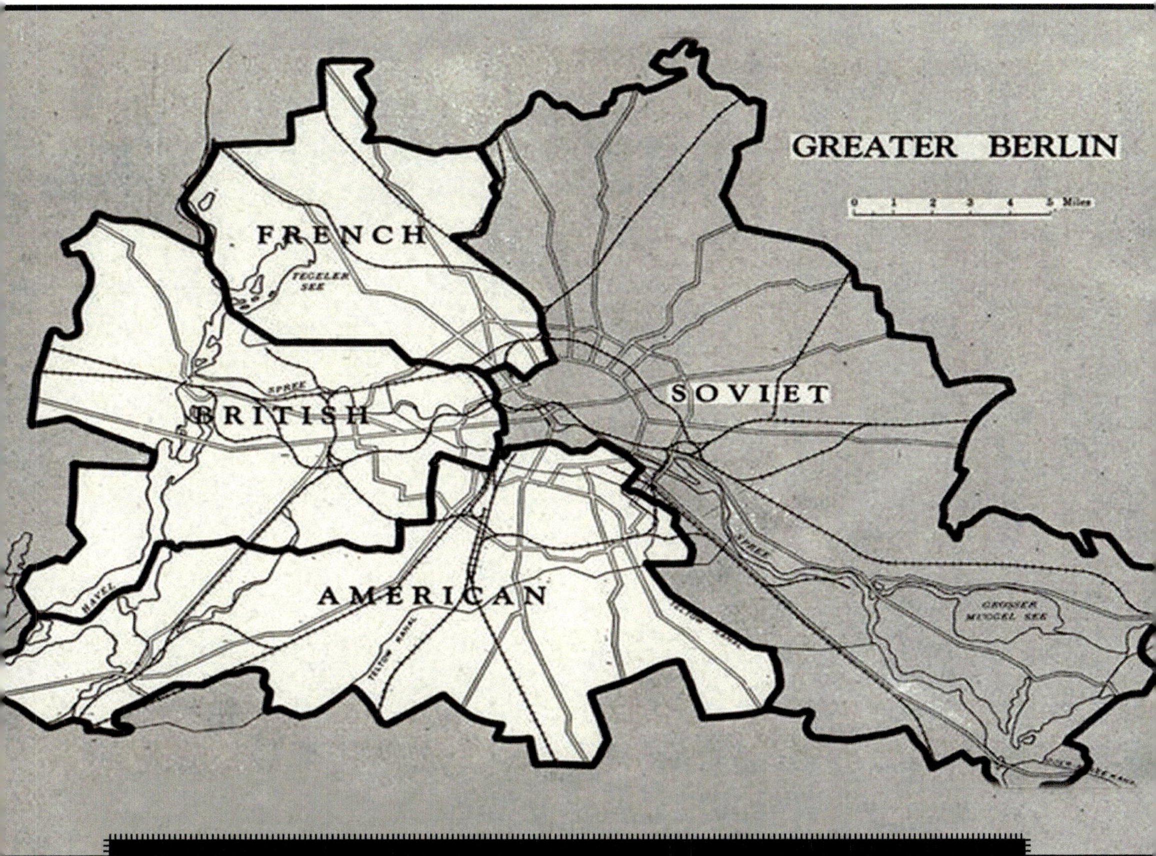

This map shows the Berlin Blockade (June 24, 1948–May 12, 1949), one of the Cold War's first major international crises. During it, the Soviets blocked railway, road, and canal access to Berlin.

The Soviets went on to establish Communist governments in other Eastern European countries. (Since then, many of these countries have been reorganized and renamed.) In his 1946 "Iron Curtain" speech, British prime minister Winston Churchill summed up Europe's anxieties over Stalin's intentions. Churchill said, "A shadow has fallen upon the scenes so lately lighted by the Allied victory. Nobody knows what Soviet Russia and its Communist international organization intends to do in the immediate future, or what are the limits, if any, to their expansive and proselytizing tendencies." Churchill worried that no one knew what the Soviet Union was doing in Eastern Europe. He said, "An iron curtain has descended across the Continent. Behind that line lie all the capitals of the ancient states of Central and Eastern Europe." By 1948, Stalin had placed Communists in charge of Albania, Yugoslavia, Romania, Bulgaria, Hungary, and Czechoslovakia. The USSR and the countries surrounding it became known as the Soviet bloc.

The United States feared a Communist takeover in the rest of Europe. In 1948, Great Britain, the United States, and France merged their zones to form West Germany. Stalin responded by blockading all the land routes to Berlin, cutting the city's

Wisconsin senator Joseph McCarthy stands in front of a map indicating Communist activity in the United States at a meeting on June 9, 1954, in Washington, DC.

sectors off from their national governments. The West launched a massive campaign to airdrop supplies into the city. They broke the blockade after eleven months. By this time, the United States and the USSR viewed each other as threats.

Meanwhile, Stalin and Mao discussed an alliance between their two Communist nations. In December of 1949, when China hoped to conquer the island of Formosa, Stalin refused military aid. The Cold War had begun.

THE START OF THE COLD WAR

The Cold War was a crisis in international relationships that began after World War II. Tensions between Communist and democratic nations stopped just short of warfare. Each power began an arms race.

US senator Joseph McCarthy captured the Cold War's essence in his famous "Wheeling" speech delivered in February 1950. "This is a time when all the world is split into two vast, increasingly hostile armed camps—a time of a great armaments race. Today we can almost physically hear the mutterings and rumblings of an invigorated god of war."

Prodded by McCarthy, the United States government took measures against anyone associated with Communism. Small Communist parties had existed in the United States since 1919. Nonetheless, McCarthy believed they threatened democracy. The House Un-American Activities Committee (HUAC), formed in 1938, investigated suspected Communists through the 1940s and 1950s. People accused of Communist involvement lost their jobs or went to prison, although many were innocent. Senator Joseph McCarthy even accused officials within the US government of being Communists.

The Truman Doctrine of 1947 authorized US support for any nation threatened by Soviet expansion. The United States used

This is the report of President Harry S. Truman's address to Congress on March 12, 1947. Truman established what became known as the Truman Doctrine, American foreign policy to obstruct Soviet efforts to expand Communism worldwide.

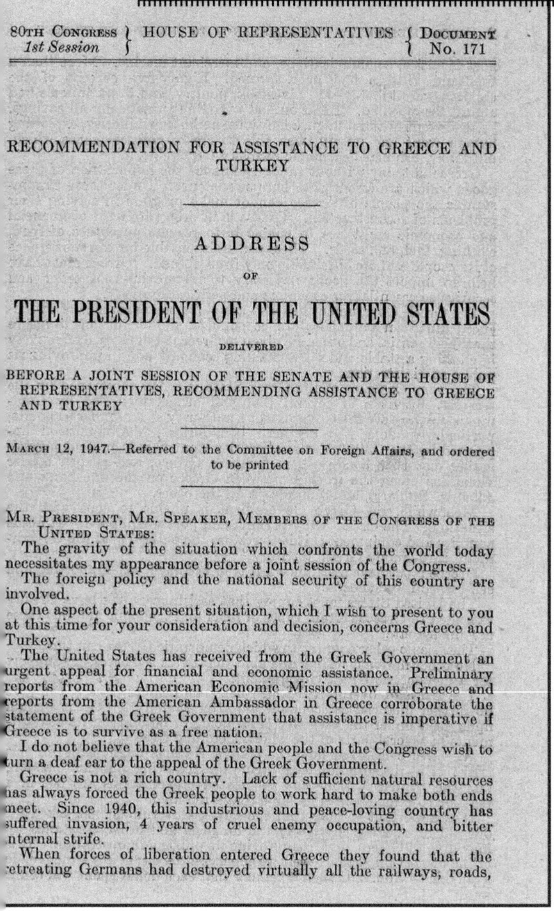

80TH CONGRESS, 1st Session | HOUSE OF REPRESENTATIVES | DOCUMENT No. 171

RECOMMENDATION FOR ASSISTANCE TO GREECE AND TURKEY

ADDRESS

OF

THE PRESIDENT OF THE UNITED STATES

DELIVERED

BEFORE A JOINT SESSION OF THE SENATE AND THE HOUSE OF REPRESENTATIVES, RECOMMENDING ASSISTANCE TO GREECE AND TURKEY

MARCH 12, 1947.—Referred to the Committee on Foreign Affairs, and ordered to be printed

MR. PRESIDENT, MR. SPEAKER, MEMBERS OF THE CONGRESS OF THE UNITED STATES:

The gravity of the situation which confronts the world today necessitates my appearance before a joint session of the Congress.

The foreign policy and the national security of this country are involved.

One aspect of the present situation, which I wish to present to you at this time for your consideration and decision, concerns Greece and Turkey.

The United States has received from the Greek Government an urgent appeal for financial and economic assistance. Preliminary reports from the American Economic Mission now in Greece and reports from the American Ambassador in Greece corroborate the statement of the Greek Government that assistance is imperative if Greece is to survive as a free nation.

I do not believe that the American people and the Congress wish to turn a deaf ear to the appeal of the Greek Government.

Greece is not a rich country. Lack of sufficient natural resources has always forced the Greek people to work hard to make both ends meet. Since 1940, this industrious and peace-loving country has suffered invasion, 4 years of cruel enemy occupation, and bitter internal strife.

When forces of liberation entered Greece they found that the retreating Germans had destroyed virtually all the railways, roads,

the Truman Doctrine of countering Soviet expansion to justify fighting Mao-supported Communist forces during the Korean War from 1950 through1953. The war ended in a stalemate. Korea split into two halves: Communist North Korea and democratic South Korea.

China and the Soviet Union also supported successful Communist revolutions in Cambodia and Vietnam, despite American involvement in the Vietnam War from 1959 to 1973.

Communism soon spread through Central and South America. Fidel Castro led a successful revolution against Cuban dictator General Fulgencio Batista from 1953 to 1959. He established a Communist government in Cuba.

Soviet scientists developed an atomic bomb shortly after Stalin's death in 1953. The arms race between the United States and the Soviet Union escalated.

In 1962, the USSR installed missiles capable of carrying nuclear weapons in Cuba. The Cuban Missile Crisis caused a panic in the United States. Tense negotiations between the

CUBA AND CASTRO

Fidel Castro led a successful revolution against Cuban dictator General Fulgencio Batista from 1953 to 1959. Castro established a Communist government in Cuba. Led by Dr. Fidel Castro Ruz and the Argentinian-born Dr. Ernesto "Che" Guevara, the revolutionaries seized US-owned businesses without compensating the owners. The United States broke off diplomatic relations and launched the unsuccessful Bay of Pigs invasion in 1961. Under Castro's guidance, Cuba began a program of radical land reform, nationalized industries, and enacted universal health care. The United States instituted a political and economic blockade against the island nation in 1962. Castro retaliated by strengthening his country's relationship with the USSR.

nations followed, ending when the USSR removed the missiles. In exchange, the United States promised not to invade Cuba. In his "Universal Conscience" speech, delivered in 1968, Castro expressed frustration at being used as a pawn during the crisis. "What really caught our attention was the fact that, when peace was truly endangered, when the world was on the brink of a nuclear war, we did not see mass mobilizations in Europe."

The Soviet Union angered the international community in 1979 by invading Afghanistan. The move soured improving relations with the United States. The Soviet economy began to suffer. High prices for natural resource exports kept the USSR's economy afloat through the 1970s, but prices soon fell. No outside markets existed for Soviet manufactured goods. The war in Afghanistan depleted cash reserves. It dragged on until 1989, ending in an embarrassing defeat for the Soviet army.

Mikhail Gorbachev, General Secretary of the Communist Party of the Soviet Union, attends the 10th Congress of the Polish United Workers' Party (a Communist group) in June 26, 1986.

Mikhail Gorbachev became general secretary of the USSR in 1985. He began the policies of Glasnost (openness) with the media and Perestroika (restructuring) within the government and economy. Gorbachev's reforms disrupted the economy, causing shortages. Party leaders urged him to slow his reforms.

Gorbachev left Soviet bloc nations to govern themselves. Many reform governments ousted their Soviet leaders. The most dramatic instance occurred in Germany. In 1961, the Soviet leader Nikita Khrushchev had ordered a wall built through Berlin. The wall separated the Soviet side of the city from democratic West Berlin. On November 9, 1989, East Germans began tearing down the Berlin Wall.

Gorbachev and the weakened USSR could not stop the independence movements. Vaclav Havel, elected president of Czechoslovakia in 1989, announced his views on Communism's decline in a speech given in 1990:

> The previous regime—armed with its arrogant and intolerant ideology—reduced man to a force of production and nature to a tool of production. In this it attacked both their very substance and their mutual relationship. It reduced gifted and autonomous people, skillfully working in their own country, to nuts and bolts of some monstrously huge, noisy, and stinking machine, whose real meaning is not clear to anyone. It cannot do more than slowly but inexorably wear down itself and all its nuts and bolts.

A failed coup attempt by members of the military in 1991 marked the end of Gorbachev's reign. He resigned afterward, leaving the government to Boris Yeltsin. Yeltsin dissolved the Communist Party. He and the heads of the Ukraine and Belorussia declared the Soviet Union defunct. All residual functions of the Soviet Union stopped on December 31, 1991. The USSR faded out of existence.

MODERN COMMUNISM

Since the Soviet Union's fall, few Communist countries remain. The People's Republic of China, North Korea, Vietnam, and Cuba make up the list of surviving Communist governments.

In December 2011, Kim Jon Il the leader of North Korea, and the son of its founder, died. His son Kim Jong-Un became the country's supreme leader. Tensions rose between North Korea, South Korea, and the United States. North Korea repeatedly

Members of the North Korean military mark the anniversary of founder Kim Il Sung's birth. Behind them stand the bronze statues of forner leaders Kim Il Sung (*left*) and Kim Jong Il (*right*).

threatened both countries with nuclear and ballistic missile attacks. A North Korean intercontinental ballistic missile test in July 2017 indicated that it could reach the United States. However, in April 2018, both Kim and President Trump indicated a willingness to hold a summit to explore a reduction in tensions.

Communist parties still thrive across the globe, though most no longer reach for worldwide revolution. Instead, they form coalition parties with other groups and work for causes they believe in. Despite the stigma attached to Communist government by the policies of Stalin and Mao, many are still willing to answer Marx's rallying call: "Workingmen of all countries, unite!"

TIMELINE

375–370 BCE Plato writes *Republic*.

1516 Thomas More publishes his influential book *Utopia*.

1799 Robert Owen buys several mills in New Lanmark, Scotland, and begins building utopian communities.

1847 The Communist League commissions Karl Marx and Friedrich Engels to write *The Communist Manifesto*.

1871 The French army puts down the Paris Commune.

1905 The Revolution of 1905 begins in Russia.

1917 Vladimir Lenin overthrows Russia's government and installs the first Communist national government.

1922 The USSR is founded.

1924 Joseph Stalin assumes control of the USSR.

1928 Stalin implements the Five-Year Plan.

1931 Mao Tse-tung begins a Communist uprising in China.

1953 Soviet scientists develop the atomic bomb.

1959 Fidel Castro's Communist movement overthrows the Cuban government.

1961 The Soviet Union builds the Berlin Wall, dividing East and West Berlin.

1962 The Cuban Missile Crisis takes place.

1968 The Soviet army invades Czechoslovakia to end the Prague Spring movement.

1985 Mikhail Gorbachev becomes USSR general secretary.

1989 East Germans tear down the Berlin Wall.

1991 The USSR is officially declared defunct.

MARX, KARL, AND FRIEDRICH ENGELS. *THE COMMUNIST MANIFESTO*. 1848.

Transcription Excerpt

A specter is haunting Europe–the specter of Communism. All the powers of old Europe have entered into a holy alliance to exorcise this specter.

But whatever form they may have taken, one fact is common to all past ages, viz., the exploitation of one part of society by the other. No wonder, then, that the social consciousness of past ages, despite all the multiplicity and variety it displays, moves within certain common forms, or general ideas, which cannot completely vanish except with the total disappearance of class antagonisms.

In short, the Communists everywhere support every revolutionary movement against the existing social and political order of things.

In all these movements they bring to the front, as the leading question in each case, the property question, no matter what its degree of development at the time.

Finally, they labor everywhere for the union and agreement of the democratic parties of all countries.

The Communists disdain to conceal their views and aims. They openly declare that their ends can be attained only by the forcible overthrow of all existing social conditions. Let the ruling classes tremble at a Communist revolution. The proletarians have nothing to lose but their chains. They have a world to win.

Workingmen of all countries, unite!

LETTER FROM LENIN TO MEMBERS OF THE POLITBURO, MARCH 19, 1922.

Transcription Excerpt

Copy To Comrade Molotov

Top Secret For members of the Politburo

We must pursue the removal of church property by any means necessary in order to secure for ourselves a fund of several hundred million gold rubles (do not forget the immense wealth of some monasteries and lauras) ... But to do this successfully is possible only now. All considerations indicate that later on we will fail to do this, for no other time, besides that of desperate famine, will give us such a mood among the general mass of peasants that would ensure us the sympathy of this group, or, at least, would ensure us the neutralization of this group in the sense that victory in the struggle for the removal of church property unquestionably and completely will be on our side ... we must precisely now smash the Black Hundreds clergy most decisively and ruthlessly and put down all resistance with such brutality that they will not forget it for several decades.

QUOTATION FROM CHAIRMAN MAO TSE-TUNG'S ESSAY, "ON NEW DEMOCRACY" (JANUARY 1940).

Transcription Excerpt

Communism is at once a complete system of proletarian ideology and a new social system. It is different from any other ideological and social system, and is the most complete, progressive, revolutionary and rational system in human history. The ideological and social system of feudalism has a place only in the museum of history. The ideological and social system of capitalism has also become a museum piece in one part of the world (in the Soviet Union), while in other countries it resembles 'a dying person who is sinking fast, like the sun setting beyond the western hills,' and will soon be relegated to the museum. The Communist ideological and social system alone is full of youth and vitality, sweeping the world with the momentum of an avalanche and the force of a thunderbolt.

GLOSSARY

AMBASSADOR A diplomat who represents his or her country's government while dealing with other nations.

ARMS RACE A competition between nations to have the most powerful stock of weapons.

BLOC A combination of nations with common interests.

CAPITAL A part of the proceeds of industry, which can either support human beings or assist in production.

CAPITALIST One who practices capitalism, the economic system based on private and corporate ownership of goods and business rather than state control.

COLONIZATION A country's practice of sending out groups of people to live and work in territory outside of their home nation.

COMMENTARY A record or explanation of events.

COMMUNAL Shared by members of a community, especially when property is collectively owned.

CORNERSTONE A basic element, or foundation, of a policy.

CZAR A monarch who ruled the Russian Empire before the October Revolution of 1917. Also spelled "tsar."

EXPLOITATION Improper use of another person or group for selfish purposes.

IDEALISTIC Placing beliefs before practical considerations.

IMPERIAL Relating to or describing an empire.

INDUSTRIALIZATION To develop a country's industries on a wide scale.

LABOR UNION A group organized by workers to improve members' wages, benefits, and working conditions.

SERVITUDE The condition of being bound to service, or a lack of personal freedom.

SOVIET An elected government council in a Communist country.

SPECTRE Ghost, or something that haunts the mind. Also spelled "specter."

WAGES Payment for labor, usually on an hourly or daily basis.

YIELD To produce or provide.

FOR MORE INFORMATION

Canadian Museum of History
100 Laurier Street
Gatineau, QC K1A 0M8
Canada
(800) 555-5621
Website: http://www.historymuseum.ca
Facebook, Twitter, and Instagram: @CanMusHistory
The museum features a special exhibit on workers conditions and labor unions during the Industrial Revolution.

The Cold War Museum
Physical address:
7142 Lineweaver Road
Warrenton, VA 20187
Mailing address:
PO Box 861526
Vint Hill, VA 20187
(540) 341-2008
Email: membership@coldwar.org
Website: http://www.coldwar.org
Twitter: @ColdWarMuseum
Located at a former US Army listening post, the museum seeks to educate the public about the people, places, and events of the Cold War period, from the 1940s to the 1990s.

Communist Party of Canada
290A Danforth Avenue
Toronto, ON M4K 1N6
Canada
(416) 469-2446

Email: info@cpc-pcc.ca
Website: http://www.communist-party.ca
Facebook: @CommunistPartyOfCanada
Twitter: @compartycanada
Instagram: @Communist.party.canada
The party is dedicated to supporting Socialism for the working class. Founded in 1921, the party's ideals include freedom, fairness, and humane alternatives for the world's problems.

Communist Party USA
235 W. 23rd Street, 7th floor (Visits by appointment only)
New York, NY 10011
(212) 989-4994
Email: cpusa@cpusa.org
Website: http://www.cpusa.org
Facebook: @cpusa
Twitter: @Communistsusa
The party maintains local clubs in districts around the country. The Communist Party supports Socialism as a means of ensuring peace and equality for members of the working class.

International Socialist Organization
Website: https://www.internationalsocialist.org
Twitter and Instagram: @SocialistViews
The organization has chapters in many cities across the United States, including Los Angeles; Washington, DC; Chicago; New York; and more. It publishes the weekly *Socialist Worker* newspaper.

National Museum of American History
Smithsonian Institution
14th Street and Constitution Avenue, NW
Washington, DC
(202) 633-1000

Email: info@si.edu
Website: http://americanhistory.si.edu
Facebook: @americanhistory
Instagram: @amhistorymuseum
In addition to a collection of more than three million historical objects that includes the Star-Spangled Banner, the museum maintains an online exhibit of documents and images called "Government, Politics, and Reform."

Oakland Museum of California
Website: http://collections.museumca.org
Facebook: @museumca
Twitter and Instagram: @oaklandmuseumca
The museum includes an online exhibit of nearly twenty-five thousand political posters, including those on protest movements, unions, and community struggles.

FOR FURTHER READING

Chim, Wai. *Freedom Swimmer*. Sydney, Australia: A & U Children, 2016.

Hulick, Kathryn, and Robert Kelly. *North Korea Today*. Minneapolis, MN: Abdo Publishing, 2018.

Lee, Sungju, and Susan Elizabeth McClelland. *Every Falling Star: The True Story of How I Survived and Escaped North Korea*. New York, NY: Amulet Books, 2016.

Malaspina, Ann. *Mao Zedong and the Chinese Revolution*. New York, NY: Enslow Publishing, 2016.

Marx, Karl, and Friedrich Engels. *The Communist Manifesto.* Minneapolis, MN: Lerner Publishing Group, 2018.

Murphy, John. *Socialism and Communism*. New York, NY: Britannica Educational Publishing, 2015.

Perkins, Anne. *Trailblazers in Politics.* New York, NY: Rosen Publishing, 2015.

Trenton, Russell. *The Russian Revolution: The Fall of the Tsars and the Rise of Communism*. New York, NY: Britannica Educational Publishing, 2016.

Uhl, Xina M., and Jesse Jarnow. *Socialism*. New York, NY: Rosen Publishing, 2019.

Zeinert, Karen. *McCarthyism and the Communist Scare in United States History.* Berkeley Heights, NJ: Enslow Publishers, 2015.

BIBLIOGRAPHY

Associated Press. "Trump Floats Korean DMZ as Location for Summit with Kim Jong Un." *Los Angeles Times*, April 30, 2018. http://www.latimes.com/world/la-fg-trump-north-korea-dmz-20180430-story.html.

Borkenau, Franz. *World Communism*. Ann Arbor, MI: University of Michigan Press, 1978.

"Domino Theory." A+E Networks, 2009. https://www.history.com/topics/cold-war/domino-theory.

Hobsbawm, Eric. *The Age of Extremes: A History of the World, 1914–1991*. New York, NY: Pantheon Books, 1994.

Oglesby, Carl, ed. *The New Left Reader*. New York, NY: Grove Press, Inc., 1969.

Owen, Robert. *A New View of Society and Other Writings*. New York, NY: Penguin Books, 1991.

Ozinga, James R. *Communism: The Story of the Idea and Its Implementation*. Englewood Cliffs, NJ: Prentice-Hall, Inc., 1987.

Schrecker, Ellen. *The Age of McCarthyism: A Brief History with Documents*. New York, NY: St. Martin's Press, 1994.

Trotsky, Leon. *The First 5 Years of the Communist International, Vol. 1*. New York, NY: Pathfinder Press, 1972.

Tse-tung, Mao. *Four Essays on Philosophy*. Peking, China: Foreign Languages Press, 1968.

Tucker, Robert C., ed. *The Marx-Engels Reader.* New York, NY: W. W. Norton and Company, 1978.

INDEX

V

W

Y

Z

ABOUT THE AUTHORS

Xina M. Uhl discovered her love of history while still in grade school. She went on to obtain a master of arts in history from California State University, Northridge. After teaching college-level American history, she moved into educational writing. She has authored books, textbooks, teachers' guides, lessons, and assessment questions in the field of history. When she is not writing or reading, she enjoys travel, photography, and hiking with her dogs. Her blog features her travel adventures and latest fiction projects.

Theodore Link is a writer who lives in Chicago, Illinois.

PHOTO CREDITS

Cover (*Communist Manifesto*) DEA Picture Library/De Agostini /Getty Images; cover (Marx), p. 32 Bettmann/Getty Images, cover (Berlin wall) Patrick Piel/Gamma-Rapho/Getty Images; pp. 5, 9, 12, 22, 44 Hulton Archive/Getty Images; p. 7 DEA/G. Dagli Orti/DeAgostini/Getty Images; pp. 15, 43 Universal History Archive/Universal Images Group/Getty Images; pp. 16, 25, 27, 34, 37 Library of Congress Prints and Photographs Division; p. 17 image courtesy of Bibliothek der Friedrich-Ebert-Stiftung, Bonn, Germany; p. 28 Mondadori Portfolio/Getty Images; p. 30 Library of Congress Exhibitions, Revelations from the Russian Archives, www.loc.gov/exhibits/archives/intn.html#obj10; p. 46 National Archives and Records Administration; p. 48 Wojtek Laski/Hulton Archive/Getty Images; p. 50 Kyodo News/Getty Images; chapter opener pages (world map silhouette) Vectorios2016/DigitalVision Vectors/Getty Images.

Design and Layout: Nicole Russo-Duca; Photo Researcher: Nicole DiMella